HILLSBOROUGH
20 YEARS ON

For all you need to know about what
really happened at Hillsborough and
the aftermath visit:
www.hfdinfo.com

First Published 2009 by Countyvise Limited,
14 Appin Road, Birkenhead, Wirral CH41 9HH

Copyright © 2009 Mike Bartram and contributors
The right of Mike Bartram to be identified as the editor of this work
has been asserted by him in accordance with the Copyright, Design
and Patents Act 1988.

The rights of the individual authors to be identified as the author
of their work has been asserted by them in accordance with the
Copyright, Design and Patents Act 1988.

British Library Cataloguing in Publication Data.

A catalogue record for this book is available from the British Library.

ISBN 978 1 906823 15 3

In Remembrance

John Alfred Anderson (62)
Colin Mark Ashcroft (19)
James Gary Aspinall (18)
Kester Roger Marcus Ball (16)
Gerard Bernard Patrick Baron (67)
Simon Bell (17)
Barry Sidney Bennett (26)
David John Benson (22)
David William Birtle (22)
Tony Bland (22)
Paul David Brady (21)
Andrew Mark Brookes (26)
Carl Brown (18)
David Steven Brown (25)
Henry Thomas Burke (47)
Peter Andrew Burkett (24)
Paul William Carlile (19)
Raymond Thomas Chapman (50)
Gary Christopher Church (19)
Joseph Clark (29)
Paul Clark (18)
Gary Collins (22)
Stephen Paul Copoc (20)
Tracey Elizabeth Cox (23)
James Philip Delaney (19)
Christopher Barry Devonside (18)
Christopher Edwards (29)
Vincent Michael Fitzsimmons (34)
Thomas Steven Fox (21)
Jon-Paul Gilhooley (10)
Barry Glover (27)
Ian Thomas Glover (20)
Derrick George Godwin (24)
Roy Harry Hamilton (34)
Philip Hammond (14)
Eric Hankin (33)
Gary Harrison (27)
Stephen Francis Harrison (31)
Peter Andrew Harrison (15)
David Hawley (39)
James Robert Hennessy (29)
Paul Anthony Hewitson (26)
Carl Darren Hewitt (17)
Nicholas Michael Hewitt (16)
Sarah Louise Hicks (19)
Victoria Jane Hicks (15)
Gordon Rodney Horn (20)
Arthur Horrocks (41)

Thomas Howard (39)
Thomas Anthony Howard (14)
Eric George Hughes (42)
Alan Johnston (29)
Christine Anne Jones (27)
Gary Philip Jones (18)
Richard Jones (25)
Nicholas Peter Joynes (27)
Anthony Peter Kelly (29)
Michael David Kelly (38)
Carl David Lewis (18)
David William Mather (19)
Brian Christopher Mathews (38)
Francis Joseph McAllister (27)
John McBrien (18)
Marion Hazel McCabe (21)
Joseph Daniel McCarthy (21)
Peter McDonnell (21)
Alan McGlone (28)
Keith McGrath (17)
Paul Brian Murray (14)
Lee Nicol (14)
Stephen Francis O'Neill (17)
Jonathon Owens (18)
William Roy Pemberton (23)
Carl William Rimmer (21)
David George Rimmer (38)
Graham John Roberts (24)
Steven Joseph Robinson (17)
Henry Charles Rogers (17)
Colin Andrew Hugh William Sefton (23)
Inger Shah (38)
Paula Ann Smith (26)
Adam Edward Spearritt (14)
Philip John Steele (15)
David Leonard Thomas (23)
Patrik John Thompson (35)
Peter Reuben Thompson (30)
Stuart Paul William Thompson (17)
Peter Francis Tootle (21)
Christopher James Traynor (26)
Martin Kevin Traynor (16)
Kevin Tyrrell (15)
Colin Wafer (19)
Ian David Whelan (19)
Martin Kenneth Wild (29)
Kevin Daniel Williams (15)
Graham John Wright (17)

20 Years On

It's now been 20 years, and in that passing of time
Do you realise those young boys would be men now,
some of them even in their prime?
And those girls could now be mothers, with children
one, two or three.
Has what you've done sunk in yet?
The suffering you've caused, can't you see?

Contents

Foreword

I am pleased to be able to write the foreword to this book of poems on behalf of the Hillsborough Justice Campaign. The initiative to write and collate these poems arose directly from supporters and is a fine example of how strength of feeling over Hillsborough motivates and translates into positive action.

The events of the 15th April 1989 at the Hillsborough Stadium, Sheffield, led to the deaths of 96 Liverpool supporters as well as hundreds of injured fans. The true consequences and trauma of that day however, extend beyond the physical to an inestimable number of people who were greatly affected by the Disaster.

Twenty years on, it is possible to view Hillsborough through various 'phases'. The immediate disaster incorporated emotions of pain and disbelief as well as anger and hurt at the inflammatory headlines in the media which sought to victim blame; an interim period of hope was experienced when it was thought by many that the legal system would hold accountable those responsible for the disaster; long term, the system failed people and a variety of reactions occurred. Some people appeared resigned to the fate of injustice, others vowed to fight on and campaign for a justice deserved, and some, wrote poems...

From the early days of the disaster there have been those that have used poetry as a vehicle for their emotions ("Words of Tribute" probably being the first). Poems written in those early days range from people's experiences of the day, to tributes from those who wished to pay their respects to the dead. Twenty years on, this volume of poetry, whilst containing poems written in 1989, also includes a reflective element that only time allows and is illustrative of views and emotions over time.

Some of the poems highlight the events of the 15th April 1989 and as a consequence pay tribute to the brave fans who acted as rescuers while police stood idly by. The imagery in some of these poems is immensely powerful, for example:

The men with impossible arms saved many more lives on that day

This is clearly a reference to those who saved lives pulling people from the pens either up into the stands or out of the crush.

Other poems speculate as to a different legal outcome had police died instead of fans:

Imagine the uproar and the weight of the law if 96 coppers lay dead on the floor.

The passing of time does little to ease the pain for many:

17 years and it hurts no less.

The deeply entrenched hatred for a particular newspaper is a recurring theme in many of the poems:

Nearly 20 years on...never ever...forgive it... continue to boycott the S*n.

Though varied in content and opinion, nevertheless these poems collectively offer the reader a fine example of the strength of feeling retained by people in respect of Hillsborough. For twenty years people have experienced loss, suffering and an overwhelming injustice. A failure to be heard in the legal arena has led to many finding a different outlet for their testimonies – through poetry. It is in this manner that the poems should be viewed. These poems are both an example of survivors reclaiming moral ownership of their lived experiences and also a testimony to the enduring power of truth through the written word. Twenty years on, what better tribute to the 96 dead of Hillsborough?

Sheila Coleman
2009

Hillsborough 20 Years On

Hillsborough

Of all 96, I knew not one name.
Yet the arguments go on, just the same.
How and why did 96 people die,
Leaving families to weep and cry?

Their need for JUSTICE must not fail
Indeed it's become a Holy Grail.
The rest of the world must now be told
That 'hillsborough' as yet is only on hold.

Until at last the truth will have its day
their families will never go away.
Minutes, hours, days, weeks, months and years
Through all the heartache and the tears

The people left behind will fight
Because that is their given right.
For the loved ones that they lost
Someone, somewhere has to count the cost,

The cost of lives cut down in their prime
Their memory remembered for all time
On that day someone was to blame
For the 96 who died at that game.

'Hillsborough' will never go away,
Until someone or organisation is made to pay
For that terrible destruction of human life.
Nothing but JUSTICE will end the strife.

Gerry McIver

The Wait For Tickets

The wait for tickets for the game.
The wait outside the Leppings Lane.
The wait to chant and sing and shout.
The wait to cheer and let it out.

The weight of hope inside the ground.
The weight of playing for the crowd.
The weight of bodies pressing down.
The weight of guilt in a bizzie's frown.

The wait at home for final score.
The wait at home for the front door.
The wait to hear a loved one phone.
The wait to see them safe at home.

The weight of a copper's boot on the path.
The weight of knuckles rat tat tat.
The weight of grief a city feels.
The weight of tears could fill Anfield.

The wait for Truth to be made plain.
The wait for courts to ease the pain.
The wait for tawdry politics.
We want Justice For The 96.

MichaelA

Me Best Mate

what's the point
does anybody care
is there anyone left
who was actually there

on that very sad day
when I lost some of me mates
how many of you can remember
that very special date

when they went out on a Saturday
to watch a game that's all
it was the FA Cup semi final
just another game of football

it didn't have to happen
didn't need to end this way
just after 3 o'clock
on that fateful Saturday

these days most folk don't remember
it's just a piece of old news from the past
a question in a trivia quiz
two points, it won't last

but the memory is still out there
it still stands out for real
justice still awaits
those 96 lives on appeal

the truth has not yet been told
to the world through the global media
too many lies and guesses
in the media circus encyclopaedia

but one thing is for sure
I'll always remember the date
it was April 15th 1989
the day I lost me best mate...

Johnlemmon

Look After Them Shanks

It promised to be a great day out
Wembley next was the shout
Unaware of what lay ahead
Father decked son out all in red
Red and white 3 lanes wide
The mass migration of Merseyside
The sun was up and laughter flowing
Who could have ever doubted going?
I watched from a distance - Row 48
It all hit home far far too late
One mate next to me, 3 down below
Alive or dead I just didn't know
We all came through and for that we give thanks
And of the 96 others?
....Look after them Shanks

Seanbren

Ever Seen?

Ever seen a magician, all illusions and tricks?
Ever seen a con man, setting up a fix?
Remember Redford and Newman, and how
they pulled off a sting?
Nothing but smoke and mirrors, enjoyment to
bring.

Ever seen a police force lie in court?
The best justice system in the world!
ha.. perish the thought.
Ever seen a whitewash ever that white?
Ever seen corruption show such strength and
might?

Ever seen a liar show no fear in his eyes?
Ever seen a rag produce such lies?
Ever seen a 'kiss off' avoided that way?
I never have and never will, until my dying day.

Mike Bartram

It Was 3 O'Clock Kick Off

It was 3 0'clock kick off, the whistle had gone,
The Kopites were singing "walk on, walk on".
The Liverpool fans were given the smaller end,
But more fans entered and the Kopites were penned.

The Liverpool fans were put in Leppings Lane.
But only to realise it would all end in pain.
As more Kopites entered, the front fans were pushed.
Many were injured but 96 crushed.

The fans screamed at Grobbelaar to get some
   assistance,
But the police didn't care they just laughed from the
   distance.
The police did eventually open a gate.
But by the time it was open it was all too late.

Still to this day the police are to blame.
Now Liverpool has the eternal flame.
All true Kopites hate The Sun.
Because of what they have said and done.

The eternal flame will always last.
Because of the disaster in the past.
Those people who died we will never forget.
They are always in our hearts and always in our heads.

Phil

JUSTICE

Minutes of silence we share every year,
Day to day memories that bring out a tear.
Ninety-six roses laid out on the ground,
We stand back in silence, not even a sound.

The fifteenth of April in eighty nine,
Remember the place, remember the time.
Those ninety-six names and everlasting flame,
In memory of those lives, lost at "THAT" game.

A city in mourning, red and blue come to flock,
Respect paid at Anfield, they queued round the block.
The flowers, the wreaths, the poems on cards,
Red white and blue, the kop covered in scarfs.

We don't ask for much, we just want what is right,
But if justice's not done, we'll come together to fight.
Not with our fists, bats, weapons or knives,
Just united in love for those who lost lives.

Cos Scousers are people unlike any other,
We will treat an outsider as though he's a brother.
Come into our house, "d'you fancy a brew?"
Your welcome again with more people too.

Just listen to us in what we have to say,
About what happened, on that fateful spring day.
Don't just palm us off, and ignore the truth,
For there is so much to know, and so much to do.

Everyday is a chance to pass on a word,
Some wisdom, and knowledge of what you have heard.
The word that I'm using is what's wanted by us all,
It's the word that we mutter, the word that we call.

So listen now, take it in, and remember,
Pass it on to your friends, and each family member.
It's for the ninety-six friends that we all will miss,
The word we all want to hear, is the word JUSTICE.

JUSTICE for the brothers, sisters, husbands and wives,
JUSTICE for those who lost their lives.
JUSTICE for the families whose tears we share,
JUSTICE for the parents, you should know we all care.

JUSTICE is what we all fight to achieve,
JUSTICE to allow the families to finally bereave.
For the pain and the heartache they have had to endure,
JUSTICE will allow them to be angry no more.

ROPER

Sometimes

Sometimes I try to bury my thoughts
Put them out of my mind and hope they stay away
And then there's the days just like today
When you're in my head and you won't go away

I hate you for what you did that day
I hate you because its only right you should pay
You've moved on with your life not like us
You don't understand why all the fuss

You're a coward a hypocrite and a liar to boot
An inexperienced man, what exactly was your plan?

Your incompetence brought our lives to an end
And your words cut so deep the hurt will never end
But we have the strength needed to carry on
And the fight for justice will go on.

JFT96

Christine

Ferry Cross the Mersey

On the ferry, I was leaning on the rail
And the red ensign kept blowing in my face
Like a red mist.

I suddenly realised it was at half-mast
(as were all the flags in town)
And it was then the events of Saturday hit home.

Me, a Tranmere supporter, a football fan,
A Liverpudlian through and through.
I felt guilty to be alive.

David Roberts (1989)

April 15th 1989

Remember the date, it's now set in stone.

Loved ones decked in red, never came home.

Whatever the truth is we'll not likely know.

The carpet its under was swept long ago.

The people we're taught as we grow up to trust in.

Ignore all our calls for the dead to have justice.

The families' persistence is moving and right.

The police have closed ranks, but we'll carry the fight.

As days become weeks become months become years.

The Kop we will stand and remember in tears.

With strength and with honour, our Anfield home.

Justice 96, you shall never walk alone.

Marc Mendoza

Cry

Cry cry cry...
I don't know why
I still cry...
that sad day
when mates went away
I'll never know why
must be in a trance
never had the chance
to say goodbye...

So next year
I'll shed another tear
cos i will always cry
I don't know why
each day goes by
hurts more with all those lies

96 souls watching over us
no need for a fuss
to the Sc*m we can swear & cuss
Mckenzie a pile of vile puss
not one of us
I now know why
I sometimes cry
there is no reason why
so I'll just cry...

Johnlemmon

The Fences

Can you see their poor faces?
As the players tie their laces
Can you hear them scream?
The faces don't gleam

Can you hear the bones crack?
Or are you breaking their back?
The Fences were there to keep them in
Not be their metal coffin

The blue colour makes us cold
Some dead just a few years old
I don't see how we caused it
The police got us in Deep Shit

The truth on that fateful day
Was that fans permanently lay
Where police ignored pleas
And lied to reap the fees

The Fences were bent back
The cops were bloody slack
Now you say sorry
Fuck off and Watch Corrie

Sheffield's Fences have never been the same
Since that awfully fateful game
1989 was never fine
The Fences showed the death line

Matt Purchase

Memories

After 16 years the memories are clear.
Losing friends who many found dear.
To go to a football match and never return.
Now years on 96 lives never burn.

The lies that followed were too much to bear.
The S*n the Mirror it was so unfair.
An apology from those responsible was all that was asked.
To the scumbags at the S*n it was too great a task.

Memories are held for those no longer near.
Every April the 15th I shed a tear.
For the families they sadly left behind.
For the memories left all in the mind.

At three o'six take a minute out.
To remember those we cannot doubt.
To take the time to stand and try not to forget.
Of those people I miss even though I've never met.

Still today the pain will not fade away.
The tears for friends you lost that day.
Still today the pain will not fade away.
Take the time to remember the 96, on a day like today.

RIP
YNWA
Justice for the 96

Circa 1892

The Truth

"Them scousers are thieves, and robbers and such
I can't say I care for them very much.
Sure, they're quite funny in the things that they say,
But they'll probably pick your pocket that very same day."

"They're dirty, they're poor, they're always in fights,
I saw it on Harry Enfield just the other night.
I believe what I see, I believe what I read,
They're telling 'the truth', what else do I need?"

"It's a stereotype, yes. But it's hardly treason.
It wouldn't be there if there weren't any reason.
Why would someone say it if it weren't really true?
And why should I listen to someone like you?"

"I know that it's true, that place is a dive.
I know it, though I've never gone past the M25.
I know it, and what's more everyone knows.
And why do we all know it? Because the S*n told us so."

Well I am from London, I get this all the time,
And a lot can be traced back to eighty nine.
It came from a paper, who could ever dispute?
This deep web of lies, The S*n at the root.

I'll tell you the real truth, for those willing to listen,
The truth about these people you are mindlessly dissing.
Most are generous and friendly, the salt of the earth.
And the S*n is just paper, without any worth.

Mark Ballard

The Funny Thing about Justice

Imagine the uproar,
And the weight of the law,
If 96 coppers,
Lay dead on the floor.

The law could not stand this,
This terrible day,
The people who caused it,
Would be locked safe away.

The blame would be total,
And the sentence so raw,
The guilty would feel the,
Long arm of the law.

The papers would say things,
Bout' those brave lads in blue,
How did 'they' cause this?
I haven't a clue.

They were 96 heroes,
And shouldn't have died,
At least with our Justice,
We'll avenge their sweet lives.

Justice is needed,
And justice is right,
And justice is the reason,
We won't give up the fight.

We lost our brothers,
Our Sisters and Dad's
And our Mother's and Uncles,
And Friends that we had.

Yet as strange as it seems,
For that terrible day,
The justice we seeked,
Just eroded away.

We never saw Justice,
Like those brave boys in blue,
To me it seems wrong,
Does it to you?

Mike Nicholson

Shooting Star

A shooting star outside my window,
It makes my tears flow.
The rarest of sights.
I wish for your rights.
A single wish, that's all I had.
I made it for you, lad.
You were left to die that day.
We want to make them pay.
Fifteen years we've waited.
You, we've loved, them we've hated.
They slaughtered your friends.
They can never make amends.
We want them to admit they're wrong.
It's been far too long.
So my wish upon that star was this.
That the ninety six get their JUSTICE.

Rhi

Scars

When the very last flower has wilted, and there's no
more petals to drop.
Please don't think we don't care anymore, and that all
our love has come to a stop.
Some promises may appear to be broken, that seemed
unbreakable when they were made.
But our memories will last forever, you're a light that will
never fade.
And a heart doesn't have to travel, to show how much it
cares.
And a heart can remain invisible, to all the scars it bares.
Scars that run deep with anger, scars that will never fade
or heal.
Until justice is finally done, and the lies, they can no
longer conceal.

Mike Bartram

For A Liverpool Supporter I Tried To Revive

You made me promise you wouldn't die.
Now you know I told a lie.

I didn't even know your name.
I'm sorry my efforts were all in vain.

So, if you're looking down from heaven above,
You'll know I send these flowers with love.

A Sheffield Nurse (1989)

Never Give Up

Ninety six died, please never forget
Together, united, we could make a small threat
So please tell everyone, everything all the time
The S*n, the Police, those names from 89'

Because every day that passes us by
Less and less people; will start to think 'why?'
Why did they die, who was to blame?
Those South Yorkshire policeman, their heads held in shame

It's very important, that we inform all
Be big, be proud and remember 'that wall'
Those names, that wall, it's never been fair
Each day that passes by, less and less seem to care

Tell the truth, keep things real
Think of the families, how must they feel?
Their children, who died for no reason
Think of them, in this cup-winning season

So think of them, as it's to them that we owe
To inform those, who as much they not know
Pass things down, it's a race against time
Each day that goes, for this acceptable crime

There's no need to tell us, we know the score
It's the wools reading The Sun, who need our help more
Inform these people, that it's just not on
My biggest fear, the years that have gone

Seventeen years have passed, it cannot be good
I'd tell the nation, if only I could
But it's up to us; we're the little people
Who go on Sunday's, to pray at the steeple

So just think of this, when you brush it aside
Your friends and mine, ninety-six died
Keep the fight going, don't bury it under
We must make them pay, for their own blunder*

(*South Yorkshire Police you twats)

Chris

Dedicated to those men with impossible arms...

The men with impossible arms
have nothing to fear any more
they were incredibly brave that sad day
they grew up pretty quickly, that's for sure...

those men with impossible arms
were only there for the game
they did impossible things
have never since been the same...

those men with impossible arms
became heroes to me and to you
they performed unbelievable bouts of heroism
were called thugs, hooligans, yobs too...

the stupid sheep-like coppers
who stood firm as red fans were dying
"caused it all" said the filthy rag Sc*m shite
didn't worry too much about lying...

those men with impossible arms
were just so incredibly brave
as we bow down and thank them so humbly
couldn't save 96 souls from the grave...

we owe you all a debt of gratitude
as we sit here and wait for the new season
no need for guilt or doubt or remorse
you did what you did for a reason...

the men with impossible arms
saved many more lives on that day
with their selfless actions and bravery
gets my Victoria Cross come what may...

the victims are not just those who were taken
we are all victims of our own destiny throughout the ages
and those men with impossible arms
have our everlasting thanks twixt history's immortal pages...

johnlemmon

The Cover Up Begins

"I'm sorry for your loss,
But please a second of your time."
"Time will never move again,
I've lost that child of mine."

"Did your lad have tickets?"
"He had one, Leppings Lane.
I can't believe I'll never see,
His sweet young face again."

"Now one more question quickly,
Had he had a lot to drink?"
"He's ten years old, at least he was,
So how much do you think?"

"Ah, I see, your lad was ten,
He'll have had a fair few then."
"A fair few drinks? He's just a kid!"
"Did he have a drink? I'll bet he did."

"Why all these questions?"
"Well, I'll explain,
We're looking for someone,
To shoulder the blame."

"We have to keep a lid on,
The events of this day,
The truth will be silenced,
You won't have your say."

"Of course we will, we'll speak our minds."
"That's enough out of you, I don't like your kind.
We'll cover the truth with shrouds of our smoke.
Who'll listen to you? You're a national joke!"

"We've put up with stereotypes all of our lives,
Robbing scouse gits, if you believe all the lies.
But we'll fight for justice, we'll carry on with pride,
Years and years if it takes it, we won't be denied."

Nineteen years since the cover up began,
Lay the blame on the scousers - that was the plan,
Say they were rioting and out on the piss.
But we know the truth, and we WILL see justice.

Mark Ballard

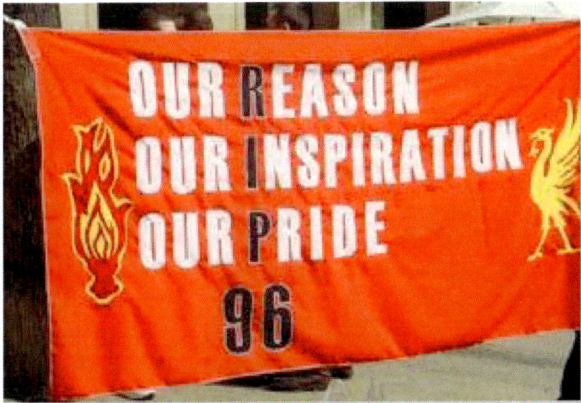

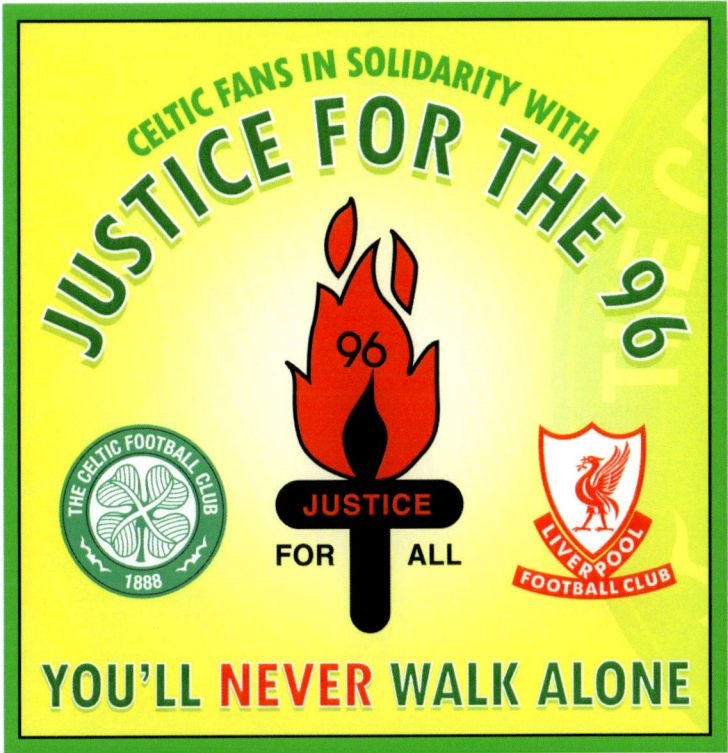

Banner Design: Ritchie Feenie (Jungle Bhoys)

Death In The Afternoon

Rosettes on the battlefield
Scarves fade as the fences shrill
frightened faces pushed in a cage
Tattooed by an iron mesh
Staring at a camera harsh
To see a death, to see a kill.

An empty ball my eye becomes
An airless lung, no last hooray
The ferryman has come for me
And why 95 die, for sweet F.A.
No cup to mourn my final day

Anon (1989)

Sorry

Sorry you say, but why are you so?
Is it cos' of the heartache down the Walton Breck Road?
Is it cos' of the mother who felt so much pain,
When her son or her daughter died in Lepping Lane?

Are you sorry because, you can't stand it to hear,
That the families were grieving, while you stabbed them
right here?
Right here in the heart, you twisted the knife,
Rubbed salt in the wound, and you shattered our life.

While Liverpool, in shock, wished back their lost sons,
You peddled your evil, told the nation we're scum.
Blood on our hands, that's what you spread,
Not a thought for the reds, there's 96 dead!

So apologise, yes, that's what we'll do,
But not on our own, well do it with Roo,
Yes we'll con a Scouse' icon, into signing for us,
Then those miserable Scousers will stop making a fuss.

They will buy our newspaper, and our profits will soar,
And about our disgrace, we'll talk no more.
That's why we're sorry, cos' we lost so much cash,
And Murdoch's not happy, as it's gone from his stash.

Fifteen long years, a million tears,
And money's the reason for all of your fears.

Mike Nicholson

Hillsborough

They waved goodbye and went their way.

Their hopes and dreams come true.

Went all the way to Sheffield,

To watch their team go through.

Stood and cheered before the game,

On telly they waved to wives.

They didn't know that later on,

They'd be struggling for their lives.

Some were pulled over, some pulled through

But the unlucky ninety-five died.

And that's when the people of Liverpool

Came together and cried.

Lindsay Carroll
St. Julie's School (1989)

"Homesick"

I miss Liverpool, the river and the ferry.
I miss all the things there that made me feel merry.
I miss Toxteth, Kingsley Road, Granby Street.
I miss reggae music's hypnotic beat.

I miss Anfield, a place of our glory.
But which last Easter told such a sad story.
All those people, so sad and down of face!
So many tears in that historic place!

I hate being stuck here, out on a limb.
Life is so competitive and often very grim.
My tears still flow at the thought of 'Home'.
I feel so lost here, virtually alone.

Up there time has helped with your grief.
But down here there is never no relief.
I suffer in a silence, oppressive and cruel.
An exiled Scouser, I miss and love you, Liverpool!

Jim

96 Stars In Heaven

Last night I saw am amazing sight,
96 extra stars burning ever so bright.
Heaven the final destination for us all,
We are just waiting the Almighty's call.
Our Lord must be creating an amazing team,
Shanks and Bob managing his great dream.
Yashin in goal, Moore at the back.
Baxter in the midfield, Dean in attack.
He is creating one mighty mix.
Roared on from the stands by our beloved ninety six.

Justice For Hillsborough.

Colin (kopite)

Get off the Pitch

I trod the turf of Hillsborough ground
I screamed at people all around:
'Please help my friends in there dying
It seems to me no-one is trying.'

The powers that be just stand and stare,
No-one to say 'Go here, go there.'
We grab the boards and start to run
Our friends are dying, one by one.

I see a policeman, ask him 'why ?'
Why is he standing idly by ?
'Get off the pitch', he said to me,
'Or you will lose your liberty.'

'Please help them, please!' I scream and shout,
'Get off the pitch, or you'll be out.'
I trod the turf of Hillsborough ground,
No more to have those friends around.

R. O'Brien (1989)

Standing On The Kop

Standing on the Kop today,
Where I have stood for twenty years.
No men in red before my eyes,
But just the mist of bitter tears.

A broken-hearted city mourns,
The dead from Sheffield's hell-hole trap.
No-one is here today to sing,
No-one is here to cheer or clap.

Ten thousand scarves before my eyes,
A hundred thousand flowers bloomed.
With words of love and tenderness,
For those whom Hillsborough's death-trap doomed.

A part of me has died today,
Along with those who suffered there.
But what I see before me now,
Must bring me hope through my despair.

I had to come and share my grief,
For ninety-six who won't be home.
Bill Shankly's arms are open wide,
With him they'll NEVER walk alone.

Chris Wood

96 in Peace

As they entered the stadium
Nobody knew what would happen
In those early Stages
Crushing against Cages

So as the police refused
The crowd got agitated
And soon People Died
Oh Relatives Cried

Many More saw the atrocity
Unfolding live on The BBC
And as 95 people slowly died
A 96th almost defied

95 became 96
The news was awful
Hillsborough 1989
Nothing will ever be fine

So the Sun tried to blame the scousers
The stupid copper who told the tabloids
Of drunk and rebellious fans
Killing whilst slurping from Beer cans

Burn the paper and Kelvin Mackenzie
Liverpool FC will never forgive
Don't buy the sun and tell your friends
This is where the Sun's legacy ends

Although 96 never returned
and the Sun was burned
The horror that unfolded that Day
Will always be remember today

15th April 1989
NOTHING WILL EVER BE FINE
GRIEF still there for the relatives
and still shock for the fans

Though some are young and weren't around
Nothing ever went sound
But when they are old enough
Tell them about the Stuff

The stuff which came from that day
Where 96 will permanently lay
Families torn apart by grief
The sun putting us into disbelief

Rest In Peace 96
Burn the Sun on Sticks
Just Rest in soft Peace
The unforgotten 96

Matt Purchase

"I'm Sorry"

When will we hear "I'm Sorry"
From the people who should feel shame
Nineteen stolen years gone by
Still no one takes the blame

The bible tells us to forgive
But for the families left behind
The memories of that dreadful day
Makes forgiveness hard to find

The reputation of the few
Protected at any cost
By the slander of the many
And 96 innocents lost

It seems the ends, can
by any means be justified
The course of justice altered
By conspiracy and lies

From government to media
So quick to shift the blame
From the guilty to the innocent
And responsibility disclaim

But a judgement is coming
With the guilty ones unmasked
To stand before their maker
And the question's he will ask

Will they feel the weight of guilt then
Will they finally realise
The pain the families suffered
Because of cover up and lies

May God send them straight downstairs
Where Maggie surely waits
And may they all spend eternity
Pressed up against HELLS GATES.

ELDON

That Feeling

Do you ever get that feeling, just like the one that I've
had today.
That something is eating away at your soul, and then
cruelly spitting it away.
That feeling that something will eat you up, until it
eventually swallows you whole.
Well that's the way I feel about justice, and it's a feeling
that I can't control.
Do you ever feel frustrated, when nothing seems to be
getting done?
That everything will soon be discarded, forgotten like a
burnt out sun.
If you ever get these feelings, then it's time to pull
together as one.
And fight until we get that justice, cos only then will
these feelings be gone.

Mike Bartram

What will it take?

What will it take,
For justice to come,
For those 96,
Their lives now done.

Would it matter if they were 96 dead MPs?
Would it make a difference if we were to say please?
Would we see justice if the victims weren't scouse?
Would anyone claim posh kids were in a public house?

Must it be 96 soldiers lost in a war?
For people to understand the why and wherefore?
Must it be 50 dead doctors for what is deserved and is right?
Or 30 dead teachers before justice comes to light?

What about 20 dead novelists and writers?
What about 15 dead fire-fighters?
Must it be 10 people dead, protesting for peace?
Or just one single member of South Yorkshire Police?

Mark Ballard

To LFC

I thank you for the good times
And won't forget the bad
The times you made me scream with joy
The times you made me sad

You've gave me celebration
And made me cry with joy
Never have more tears been shed
Than when I was just a boy

Off to Sheffield went the boys
They went to do us proud
I remember watchin on TV
The volume turned up loud

The game began and we attacked
A roar came from the fans
What happened next will stay with me
Had me weeping in my hands

I won't go into detail here
I can't, it makes me cry
We all know what happened there
What we don't know is why

The next day amid all the tears
My first li'l bro was born
I couldn't feel true happiness
My heart felt like it was torn

Like his dad, he chose the blue
Despite his date of birth
But at the tender age of 7
he showed me his true worth

I took him down to Anfield
Explained to him the truth
Taught him about the 96
The memorial served as proof.

He ran his little finger
Down the name of each lost soul
For every name he came across
He whispered "you'll never walk alone"

Two weeks ago my baby bro
Turned 18, a baby no more
Today on May 1st he's off
To fight someone else's war

So I gotta keep me fingers crossed
An' told him to check his phone
Cos every single day I'll text
You'll never walk alone.

Lee Pascoe

For Jim & Matthew
(who came back)

I drove you up to Priory Road
To catch the coach to Hillsborough.
There was laughter.
Hopes were Derby high.
The street had flowered blue and red.

The youth of Merseyside was on the move,
Plastic bags in hand.
Butties packed by loving mums and wives.
Such precious lives.

I drove you back to Anfield.
The Kop was draped in blue and red,
Across the pitch, the flowers had spread,
Like Flanders field, for youth now dead.

Shirley Tomlinson (1989)

17 Years

17 years and it hurts no less.
Like just yesterday when my thoughts regress.
Blocking out more than I can recall.
For my mind can't handle the horror in full.

Grieving was stifled by incomprehension.
We held hands in the cathedral amidst insane tension.
I asked my family and God of this 'blunder.'
How death of his 'children' could be part of his 'wonder'.

My heart's got no answer and I don't think it will.
As press climbed on board and 'hacked' further still.
Our grief was raw our hearts angry and wild.
But the scum chose to lie and our grief was defiled.

There've been no such events in which we've had to deal.
With the pain and the hurt we all every day feel.
We lost our brothers and sisters on this the 15th day.
Do you blame me still for wanting someone to say
.... SORRY?

Glorious Future

Justice For All

Those 96, forever Red.
In my heart and in my head.
Across the Pennines that fateful day.
Whilst dreams abound of Wembley Way.

Red and white, songs and cheers.
Programmes, scarves and souvenirs.
Tears and heartache, crushing pain.
Left to rot on Leppings Lane.

"Five to three, open that gate!"
"THEY STOLE FROM THE DEAD WHEN THEY TURNED UP
LATE!"
That stuff they wrote, it made us cry.
"THE TRUTH" they said when telling lies.

And all of this to watch a game.
We get no justice, just our flame.
With those 96 we'll be as one.
We won't forget - don't buy The S*n.

Allan

Colours

The Red Scarf lies on the Green Grasses
The Redtop rag lies to the buying masses
The Black and White letters spelt out shit
Whilst the Blue Police sold it.

The grass has grown above those who died
as do the numbers who despise the rag that lied.

Michael Hines

For You This Christmas

A Christmas 96 innocent people will never see.
Some lead a selfish Christmas, and that includes me.
But if you can spare a moment, and find the time.
Then remember the 96, and these few words of mine.

96 fans all dressed in red, no more winters to be seen.
And nobody had the right, to take away their every
dream.
But take them away they did, and yet nobody has yet to
pay.
For the lives they took and ruined, on that fateful April
day.

So from when you put up your trees, until they come
down all barren and bare.
Spare a thought for our lost friends, and show them that
you care.
Or think of them in heaven, looking down on us from
above.
So this Christmas I dedicate to the 96, from me to you
with love.

Mike Bartram

Easy to Forget

It's easy to forget in this joyous time,
what happened back then in '89.
I myself was only 3,
not old enough to remember the carnage and misery.
You'll think, why does he care?
He wasn't even there,
No friends or relatives lost,
you haven't felt the cost.
I don't see it that way,
I care about what happened on that fateful day.
I care about something I didn't even see,
Because I know, 10 years before,
It could have been me.
Now I'm part of the greatest family,
The club that is Liverpool FC
In 89, 96 loyal reds,
Went to see a semi-final of the cup,
Not knowing that they're never see their beds,
That is why we must never give up,
We all go to the game,
Otherwise it wouldn't be the same,
We see the eternal flame burn,
But do we ever think, we might never return?
In a world of plastic seats and Sky TV,
It's easy to forget,
That those 96 were just like you and me.
That is why as the years roll on,
No matter how much we've won,
We must never forget those 96 names,
Who can no longer go to games.

Tom Johnson

My Beloved Crowd

Every week I watched my team.
The Spion Kop the famous scene.
We scored a goal the voices roared
For any player in Red who scored.

The bond between the fans was great.
As people passed the Shankly Gate.
90 minutes we would boo and cheer
Opposition shook with fear.

FA Cup Semi-Final day.
Didn't need our tickets nothing to pay.
A crowd of Red and White.
In the stand all filled with fright.

Went down with FIVE in a car
NEVER went to a public bar.
We arrived at the ground our little crew
Sunday morning came home with TWO.

I'll miss you lads you were sound
I've laid flowers on our home ground.
Another match I'll never go
My beating heart has sunk so low.

Ta ra boys.

Jason Quinn

Dedicated to the Liverpudlians

Scousers were looking forward to the semi-final game,
At Hillsborough and Villa, it should have been the same.
We weren't aware and we hadn't heard a thing -
Didn't know the horrors a day like that could bring.

At four forty-five, as we left the ground.
There was no jubilation, hardly a sound.
We left for home, not a word was said.
As over the radio it was "eighty-four dead."

I shook my head, and froze in pure disbelief.
My fellow Evertonians all shared in the grief.
We feel for each person, family or friend -
How I wish all their suffering torment could end.

All the broken hearts and shattered lives
That this terrible day has brought.
You'll never walk alone, my friends.
You'll always have our support.

A. Bromilow,
A broken-hearted Evertonian, April 1989

Red Sky at Night

Red sky at night,
Shepherd's delight,
That's way they say,
But that can't be right.

'Cos why would a shepherd.
Be delighted to see,
96 angels,
Crying with me?

Why would a shepherd,
Be happy to hear,
That 96 died,
In terror, in fear?

A Leppings Lane nightmare,
Plays again and again,
And Duckenfield caused it,
He carries the blame.

But he's off enjoying life,
While reds lay in the ground,
And not the ground of Anfield,
They don't make a sound.

So red sky at night,
Is not for the sheep,
But for 96 sons and daughters,
Who can't get any sleep.

Mike Nicholson

The 96 Looked Down

The 96 looked down
on old Athens town
and try as they might
couldn't quite reach the heights
of Istanbul
in 2005...

but ne'er fear
there's always next year
when the reds will likely be up for a game
no more Jerzy or Robbie
who'll be playing scrabble for a hobby
as we search the world for players old & new

cos to play for the reds
is an honour (he said)
as Robbie exits the front door
he sure did play good football
he gave it his all
and we may never see his like again

but for sure in his place
a centre forward will grace
our new stadium
across the park way
as the 96 looked down
on Athens with a group frown
ne'er worry
it's only on loan...

johnlemmon

For The 96

It could have been me, or it could have been you.

Or anyone you knew or loved, wearing red, white or blue.

And now many years later, no matter how hard I try.

Today's a day I can't help but cry.

And those people should never be rid of the shame.

For pointing their fingers, and shifting the blame.

I'll never forget that sunny, spring afternoon.

Or forgive those who turned a terrace into a tomb.

And now I pray as each candle is lit.

For those who once stood, where today I now sit.

Then I'll lay my red rose under the flame.

That will burn forever, in honour of their name.

Mike Bartram

There, But For The Grace Of God, Go I

Actions I could not prevent
Decision I dare not take
Results I cannot ignore
No preventions, and still no cure

A battle charge without provocation
They saw a colour, not a person
A label, not a soul
The opponent, not the needy

My own, my club, my heart, were trapped
But yet hold no reproach
Afforded no liberties; given no freedom
And without justice they remain imprisoned

YNWA

Iain

A Million Flowers

Thirteen years old,
I stood and watched,
That T.V. screen,
With my fingers crossed.

Talk of causalities,
pain and death,
I watched the News,
as I held my breath.

"Ninety-six fans at a football game,
Lost their lives today on Leppings Lane",
But the cover-up had already begun,
Between the lying filth and the dirty Sun.

We got in the car,
And went to the ground,
Thousands of people,
But barely a sound.

A carpet of flowers,
In front of our Kop,
I just stood and stared,
As though time had stopped.

I remember the crying,
I remember the dread,
As the city of Liverpool,
Mourned for its dead.

The flowers had reached the halfway line,
And I placed a bouquet at this Anfield Shrine,
At 13 years old I did not comprehend,
The importance of losing our 96 friends.

The anger came later,
When I learnt of the lies,
But for now I just stood there
And looked to the skies,

A million flowers,
A million tears,
I can't believe,
It's been 14 years.

I left my scarf near the Shankly gate,
And prayed for those who had met their fate,
96 friends we all shall miss,
And all the Kopites want Justice.

You'll Never Walk Alone.

Justice for the 96

Allan Heywood

Look Up Into The Sky...

Next time when your all alone,
Been to the pub and going home,
Look up into the sky, into the deep dark night,
Lo and behold, oh what a sight.

Look up into the sky and what can you see?
96 stars shining bright as can be,
Not any old stars twinkling away,
But the smiles of our angels taken that day.

They seem so distant, not with us no more,
Always in our hearts, for that I'm sure,
The memories, the pain, it lingers on,
But I've got a secret, I know where they've gone.

They are up in the sky, far faraway,
Discussing with Shanks "The Liverpool Way",
So next time when your all alone,
And been to the pub and going home.....

Look up into the sky......

RIP 96.
YNWA.

Tony

Flowers of Merseyside

Words alone cannot express the feelings deep inside
For families, friends and neighbours of those who died
At the Sheffield stadium on that awful April day
As they went to watch their beloved Liverpool play.

A football pitch of flowers, scarves, tears and grief,
As thousands paid their tributes in utter disbelief,
We cast off from the ferry ninety-five bouquets,
Mersey echoing our song, as the petals met the waves.

Condolences from round the world, in media and press
Mixed with those of friends and neighbours, feeling our
    distress.
We'll never forget those fallen, we'll remember them
    with pride
God took them and we don't know why, our flowers of
    Merseyside.

Mary M. Summer (1989)

I Never Knew Your Name

We've stood at games
Side by side.
We've laughed, we've sung.
We've cheered, we've cried.

We've shared the highs.
We've shared the lows.
We've even trod
On each other's toes.

When they scored a goal.
We've hugged and kissed.
We've shared a moan
When someone's missed.

We've gone off home
To meet again.
Another ground,
Another game.

But this time, where
You used to stand
There'll be a space,
we've lost a friend.

More than a friend
At L.F.C.
We were and are
One family.

On that day
I lost a brother
Son, father,
Sister, mother.

I'll miss you all
at every game.
I loved but
Never knew your name.

Linda Robinson (1989)

The Redzaar Cumin Up The Hill Boys

The redzaar cumin up the hill boys.
The redzaaar cumin up the hill boys.
All to the valley of death, we strolled in our hundreds.
Chris to the left of me, Al to the right.
Turnstiles in front of us.

Stalled in our hundreds, everyone dismayed.
No checkpoints, someone's blundered.
Ours not to make reply, ours not to reason why.
'Open the gate' came their reply.

We're on the march with Kenny's army.
We flowed in our hundreds, kopites to the left of me.
Kopites to the right of me, the dull tunnel in front of me.
Voices thundered, as the crowd began to swell.
No room to move we begin to yell.
In the jaws of death, in the mouth of hell.
Rolled in our hundreds, flashed faces in despair.
Flashed the gasps, screams for air
Bizzies just......standing there.

The game goes on while, all at home wondered.
Hands and scarves dangled in hope.
Over our heads escapes some bloke.
Kopite and kin, brake from this hold.
Moved into the sun, shattered and stunned.

Some Liverpool fans...some Liverpool fans...
All sullied, the truth plundered, justice blinded.
To the survivors and friends who tell
Just how our loved one fell.
In the jaws of death, in that mouth of hell.

While the authorities stood by, in their hundreds.
From advertising boards stretchers were made
Honour those reds who attempted first aid.
Honour those reds with truth and justice
It's the only tribute fitting for the ninety six.

Nicola Mcmillan

The Liverpool Accent

Now words refuse to say
what only hearts can speak.
The accent so renowned
For its sharp, ready wit
In those sad eyes
Becomes the accent of our grief.
Yet our true accent
Is no longer heard in speech
But felt in the depth of our being.

Drawn together, across all barriers
We reach out to each other,
Just as at Hillsborough,
The scene of our distress,
those hands reached down to lift
Up to the safety of the stand above
Any who could be rescued that way.

As arms were placed on grieving shoulders
To give some comfort, if they could.
As doors have opened, giving help to strangers,
As scarves of red and blue were linked
In that long chain
Which finds us alone together in our sorrow.

We know such signs declare,
In ways words canny say
That this is truly, at its heart,
The accent of our city.
Our 'village' city,
Where even its excited children
Will always be at home,
Together both in laughter and tears.

Wendy Ross-Barker (1989)

Move On

Same old sounds, based on the same old word.
Coming from the same song book, it's been sung,
   it's been heard.
'Why live in the past'? I've heard many times before.
'They've had their pity' some say 'and now they want
   some more'

'Where's your stiff upper lip, is your back bone weak'?
'It was 20 years ago, yet justice you still seek'
'Move on' I've heard, 'move on and let go'
'Your fight can't be won, so just deal with the blow'

But this City is proud, and it won't lie down.
We won't bow to the pressure, of stripes, stars or a
   crown.
It's answers we want, every last single one.
And when justice is ours, then we'll move on.

Mike Bartram

Justice For The 96

Whether you were there and seen it happen, or watched
   it on the news.
You know there must be justice and this I can't excuse.
There are 96 good reasons and I'll gladly name them all.
They only went to watch a game were players kicked a
   ball.

Someone hid the evidence and someone lost the tape.
People lost their lives, cos others were so late.
There's got to be a hearing, even though they say it was
   fate.
You just try to tell them that when your stood at Shankly's
Gate.

Football's detrimental when it all comes down to this.
Loving caring families couldn't give their final kiss.
It wasn't just an accident it wasn't just a miss.
The British Court of Justice have really took the piss.

Nine years of trying and still it's all in vein.
The suffering, the sadness, grief, sorrow and pain.
We will never stop fighting, we only want the truth.
We want a new enquiry to show the world the proof.

For every true supporter whose ever watched a game.
They have never seen nothing, like on the Lepping's Lane.
People can't forget it, until we have a change.
For all the wrong reasons, this match shot to fame.

Whether you support Liverpool, I couldn't really care.
Football means nothing once you seen what happened
   there.
And even if you keep your distance or live in another
   zone.
Always remember one thing, you shall never walk alone.

96 R.I.P - The fight for justice continues.

Joe Davies (true blue)

Acknowledgements

No person contributing to this book has asked for, or received, any payment for their work. Without those contributions, be it poetry, artwork, design or photography, this book would not have been possible.

So my thanks to the following for making it happen...

Sheila Coleman [HJC] for kindly writing the foreword.

Hillsborough Justice Campaign [hjcshop@tiscali.co.uk] for their support. [www.contrast.org/hillsborough]

Ritchie Feenie [Jungle Bhoys & www.250567.com] for the *Celtic Solidarity Justice* banner, and for the design of the Contents & In Remembrance pages.

Nadine Lee [www.nadineleephotography.co.uk] who took, and provided, the photographs of the Huyton Village memorial especially for this book.

Cliff Jones [Cliff Jones Fotopic] for the Kop 'Truth' mosaic photograph.

Dave Ball [©Sheffield Hallam University] for the Leppings Lane floral tribute photographs.

Mary Beth McKenna [©Sheffield Hallam University] for the Sheffield memorial photograph.

Andy Campbell for the 'Our Reason' banner photograph.

Damian Kavanagh and the lads from the village Inn for the 'Kop Justice' banner photograph.

My wife Karen, and daughters Rachel & Emma, who have been patient and taught me a lot along the way.

Finally to www.redandwhitekop.com - where the majority of poems & pictures have been collated.